HAL•LEONARD
INSTRUMENTAL
PLAY-ALONG

AUDIO
ACCESS
INCLUDED

PLAYBACK+
Speed • Pitch • Balance • Loop

ALTO SAX

STADIUM ROCK

Audio arrangements by Peter Deneff

To access audio, visit:
www.halleonard.com/mylibrary

Enter Code
3634-8912-8005-8551

ISBN 978-1-5400-7201-6

Visit Hal Leonard Online at
www.halleonard.com

Contact us:
Hal Leonard
7777 West Bluemound Road
Milwaukee, WI 53213
Email: info@halleonard.com

In Europe, contact:
Hal Leonard Europe Limited
42 Wigmore Street
Marylebone, London, W1U 2RN
Email: info@halleonardeurope.com

In Australia, contact:
Hal Leonard Australia Pty. Ltd.
4 Lentara Court
Cheltenham, Victoria, 3192 Australia
Email: info@halleonard.com.au

ALL I DO IS WIN

ALTO SAX

Words and Music by KHALED M. KHALED
T-PAIN, CALVIN BROADUS,
CHRISTOPHER BRIDGES, WILLIAM ROBERTS
JOHNNY MOLLINGS and LEONARDO MOLLINGS

Moderate Hip-Hop

CENTERFOLD

ALTO SAX

Words and Music by
SETH JUSTMAN

CRAZY TRAIN

ALTO SAX

Words and Music by OZZY OSBOURNE,
RANDY RHOADS and BOB DAISLEY

EYE OF THE TIGER

ALTO SAX

Words and Music by FRANK SULLIVAN
and JIM PETERIK

DON'T STOP BELIEVIN'

ALTO SAX

Words and Music by STEVE PERRY,
NEAL SCHON and JONATHAN CAIN

FEEL IT STILL

ALTO SAX

Words and Music by JOHN GOURLEY,
ZACH CAROTHERS, JASON SECHRIST,
ERIC HOWK, KYLE O'QUIN,
BRIAN HOLLAND, FREDDIE GORMAN,
GEORGIA DOBBINS, ROBERT BATEMAN,
WILLIAM GARRETT, JOHN HILL
and ASA TACCONE

HAVANA

ALTO SAX

Words and Music by CAMILA CABELLO, LOUIS BELL,
PHARRELL WILLIAMS, ADAM FEENEY, ALI TAMPOSI,
JEFFERY LAMAR WILLIAMS, BRIAN LEE, ANDREW WOTMAN,
BRITTANY HAZZARD and KAAN GUNESBERK

KERNKRAFT 400

ALTO SAX

By EMANUEL GUENTHER
and FLORIAN SENFTER

SANDSTORM

Words and Music by VILLE VIRTANEN
and JAAKKO SAKARI SALOVAARA

LAND OF A THOUSAND DANCES

ALTO SAX

Words and Music by
CHRIS KENNER

SEVEN NATION ARMY

ALTO SAX

Words and Music by
JACK WHITE

SWEET CAROLINE

ALTO SAX

Words and Music by
NEIL DIAMOND

WE ARE THE CHAMPIONS

Words and Music by
FREDDIE MERCURY

ALTO SAX